Sailing by Ravens

Other Books in the Alaska Literary Series

Sailing by Ravens

Holly J. Hughes

UNIVERSITY OF ALASKA PRESS

FAIRBANKS

University of Alaska Press
P.O. Box 756240
Fairbanks, AK 99775-6240

Library of Congress Cataloging-in-Publication Data

Hughes, Holly J.
 [Poems. Selections]
 Sailing by Ravens : poems / by Holly J. Hughes.
    pages cm
 ISBN 978-1-60223-225-9 (pbk. : alk. paper)— ISBN 978-1-60223-226-6
 I. Title.
 PS3608.U3586A6 2014
 811'.6--dc23
                            2013024450

This publication was printed on acid-free paper that meets the minimum
requirements for ANSI / NISO Z39.48–1992 (R2002) (Permanence of
Paper for Printed Library Materials).

In memory of Rags,
who loved the sea and always sailed by ravens.

Contents

South

E*ast*

North

Individually we are obligated to make a map
of our own homeland, our own field or meadow.
We carry engraved in our hearts the map of the world as we know it.

—James Cowan
A Mapmaker's Dream: The Meditations of Fra Mauro

The Navigational Fix

For a good fix, we need two lines, 45 degrees
apart, to meet, one leg of the dividers anchored,

the other swinging on its arc until
the lines intersect, *X* saying *here*—

this moment wrenched from time, plumbed
in place. I spread the divider's metal legs,

measure degrees in seconds, minutes, hours,
gauge *speed made good*, prick one small foot,

drag its lead twin in an arc, an easy pivot.
Then the next. Take a bearing off the lighthouse,

another arc, and where the two overlap
a sprawling *X*
                but already we've moved on.

Horizon

A daughter grows a horizon.
Somehow a line by which a life could be pursued.

—Brenda Hillman, *Cascadia*

She's not in the B&W snapshot with its deckled edge. She's the one you can't see because she's climbed out of the frame; she's made her escape out the bedroom window with its pink ruffle to the steady white pine with sap she won't wash off. Right now she hangs on with one hand; her other hand shields her eyes from the sun—she read this in *Treasure Island*—and she gazes over the muddy river valley, past the straight green rows of corn, their yellow ears sheathed. She dreams she's in the crow's nest of a ship, watching for white sails, waiting for them to fill with wind. Sails that will carry her far from here.

Captive

We each wanted to be the one to pull down
the map where it hung from a rusted bracket, to reach

with a pointer for the silver loop, a carousel ring,
then yank it down in one smooth swoop,

thrill in the unfurling, smell the musty paper,
see each country rimmed in certain black,

primary colors caged within: *Bali, Bora Bora,* the *Belgian Congo.*
Too many countries to learn by heart, but the certainty

of seven continents, seven seas, names in script:
Mediterranean, Caribbean, vast *Pacific.*

We'd wield the wooden pointer like a sword, tapping
England, France, Spain in turn. But I couldn't keep

my eyes from drifting out to the color I loved best:
blue sea holding captive all the land.

Artifacts

Villalobos, Yangtze River

Because she sails, she's given her grandfather's Navy sailor suit, his journal, B&W snapshots, the mysterious gold plaster finger, artifacts to reconstruct a history. The Boxer Rebellion. In the photos, the *Villalobos* steams up the Yangtze, shores of China remote on either side. Onboard, the sailors dine with the officers; after, volleyball on deck. Somewhere on the ship, her grandfather, a quartermaster barely eighteen, records each meal, collects postcards of what he doesn't see on shore: a string of starving Mongolian ponies; three Chinese about to be beheaded, glossy pigtails flung forward on thin necks. Somewhere ashore he came upon this gold shard of the Buddha—the finger that grounded him to this world—smuggled it back to the ship. How to make this story whole? What a generation doesn't pass along, hidden ballast the next will carry. One more life she can't know, will have to wear instead.

Desire Lines

Desire lines: where people have walked, made their own paths

About her great-grandfather, the English sea captain, she knows less. As the family story goes, the ship he commanded set sail from London, a seventeen-year-old Spanish girl of noble blood aboard bound for finishing school in Cuba. When the ship docked in New Orleans, they eloped. So much the story doesn't say. What were her first words to him, the stately captain? How many days out from port before he gazed into the vanishing horizon of her eyes? When did they stand at the bow, glimpse together a future glimmering? At what precise coordinate did they cross desire's shimmering line? Where in the vast Atlantic, as the ship steamed south, did their bodies know they would not—could not—return to the lives they'd left behind?

Desire is never on the map

it's that unnamed lake you found once, driving a gravel road,
not where you thought you were going, fast, window down,

hair loose to the dry wind, bare foot pressing metal, soft feathers
of cottonwood drifting through, maple seed spinning its wild gyre.

Bugs spatter on the windshield in Rorschach you want to read
like tea leaves, imagine you might learn how you've come

to this road, which left turn at midnight, which wrong side
of town. Then there it is glittering pure and cold before you

and suddenly you want that stone-skipping ache more
than your life, even knowing how cold water

makes each hair stand on end as you enter,
one toe at a time, sand crumbling underfoot,

then, the delicious submersion as you slip
the laws of gravity, surface tension.

And so it is you push off from shore, not caring
that this lake—as you knew the instant

you saw it—has no bottom.

Barometer

Storm's coming, my grandmother said,
days before clouds billowed above
dry Dakota plains. Even then
I wondered how she knew, what

prescient needle quivered within.
The barometer a gift for newlyweds
bound for Alaska to fish salmon.
I learned to read it every morning,

tap the clear glass twice to release
its thin needle, record in the log,
arrows pointing up or down:
29.9 falling means *storm's ahead.*

Years later would come to know
how it all turns on a molecule.

So Many Superstitions to Defy

Here you are on the *Merry Maid* our first season, the blue checked flannel shirt you would wear the next seven years still free of salmon blood. (Thirty years later, I still feel its soft heft wipe jellyfish from my eyes.) Each season, we went north with a rose in a green capers jar stuck to the window ledge with duct tape so it wouldn't topple in heavy seas. Old-timers warned *plants are bad luck,* but we ignored them, smuggled aboard a pot of basil, rosemary, thyme. So many superstitions to defy. Here, you mug for the camera, red rose clenched in your teeth. In this moment, we believe love will carry us across any sea.

Heading for Town

Here's me. I look like I'm twelve, but I'm twenty-seven. Maybe it's the upside down PFI insignia on the stained blue baseball cap. Or the salmon, a king, belly flush with eggs, blood forging tributaries down my yellow Helly Hansen bibs. Or the faded red sweatshirt, arms cut off so the wrists won't soak up fish gurry. Maybe the way I'm squinting into the sun, tired and proud. How is it I can't slip back into that frame, can't inhabit again that smelly sweatshirt? I can still conjure it all, whiff of diesel, peeling gray decks, catch and slide of the galley door, crackle of the CB. I knew it couldn't last, though nothing in my face cops to that. Still, some days there's nowhere I'd rather be, reeling like a drunk in the long swells, five nights without sleep, salmon stacked like wood in the fish hold, heading for town.

Body Memory

After a season away, my body remembers how to step over the rail, duck under the boom, glide open the wheelhouse door. Take three steps to the galley, duck again, stand up under the skylight. Knows where to stow provisions—cans of tomato sauce, chopped clams, pitted black olives, artichoke hearts—find them again, thumbs lifting wood slats from food lockers, reaching down, knowing each by heart. Stand in the stern, stomp hard on the wood pedal to bring the dripping gillnet aboard, reel it all back in as if I'd never left.

What She Can't Say

How much he drank, how much they all drank. Going north with cases of Courvoisier stacked in the hold, the finest Rothschild wines. Staggering out of the Alaskan Hotel bar at closing, stars wheeling above. *Did she see them*? That night in Sitka, herring glittering under deck lights like the cocaine glittering in crooked lines in the galley, lines that vanished over the next six hours as fifty tons of herring were scooped, shovel by shimmering shovel, into the fish hold. They skated on herring, straddled herring, swam through herring until the hold brimmed. *The rest a deck load*, skipper called, and the herring swirled on deck, fallen galaxies. *Did she see them*? Or did she see only red and green lights wink, conspiratorial, as the tender lumbered toward town, picking its way through the back channel, stars thrumming in their veins for days.

Correcting for Variation

I balance on the edge of a tall wooden stool, metal dividers splayed between my fingers, elbow pressing down the wrinkled edge of the chart. Lay the clear parallel rules across the compass rose, find 260 degrees true, swing step them across the chart to advance the track line toward Race Rocks. Now, figure rate of ebb, vessel's *speed made good, speed over ground,* like the math problems in sixth grade, where two trains leave the stations at different times—when will they collide? Convert from true to magnetic, then to a compass course, correcting for variation. The saying they taught us at Crawford Nautical School comes back: *Timid virgins make dull companions at weddings.* Heading west, add degrees. Breathe in, do the math, extend the track line with a sharp #2 pencil. Realize I'm already in deep, already about to crash.

Correcting for Deviation

Tiny bits of metal make a steady compass spin—coffee mug, sunglasses, screwdriver—each stray filing must be figured in. Ship's course not true, so ship's compass must be swung. We run a course in each direction, post a chart, account for deviation. *Steady as she goes*, but what to do when true north can't be found? How many times have the poles traded places? How many times have I, too, been swung by the moon, its elliptical orbit, all its dark phases?

What the Sea Takes, Gives Back

One day's catch recorded in the log: forty sockeye, fifteen chums, seven cohos, a white king. A receipt book, yellow pages thick as an accordion. A plastic Joy soap bottle, one tennis shoe, left, its tongue swollen. *What we keep, what we toss.* The day I dropped the fish pick overboard, watched it sink out of sight; next set, fetched up by the net. The night the storm petrel skittered down on deck, rode with us across the gulf, then flew. *What the sea takes, gives back.* The fisherman gone overboard found the next morning, boat adrift, tangled in his net.

Steer for the Light

Dark a night as I've seen,
radar small comfort in wind & rain.

A light flashes six seconds white,
green light winks off to port,

chart shows rocks all around.
Coast Pilot says, *Steer for the light,*

when you see it dead abeam,
turn the wheel hard over

to starboard, 45 degrees,
then steer for the six-second light

off the tip of Kah Shakes. I stand
behind the wheel, knees weak,

count six seconds like a mantra,
hold my course steady, darkness

slipping through my hands.

Because the sea never forgets

that night you whistled on watch,
　　　opens a thousand windows,
　　　　　slams each door shut.

Because the sea is swung
　　　by the moon,
　　　　　because the sea parts,
　　　　　　　but only for Moses.

Because the sea has no mistress,
　　　takes a thousand lovers,
　　　　　takes no prisoners,
　　　　　　　won't give up her dead.

Because the sea never gets lost
　　　promises never to tell,
　　　　　says she loves us equally,
　　　　　　　but in the end

　　　　　　　cares really not at all.

W *est*

But breath-time, heart-time, circadian,
is finer than a dotted line.

—Adrien Stoutenburg
"Dateline: Calendar Time" from *Greenwich Mean Time*

Hsui

The people   saw the Great Bear   lope
        across the night sky,   watched him   circle,
                trace an arc,   anchored to the   fixed star
                    by a glittering tail.   Watched the tail   tick

                through the dark,   the twenty-four directions,
counted them,   named each one.   On long
        winter nights, a procession of constellations,
            hsui, circled the north star.   Who first noticed

        that fixed point in the wheeling heavens?

Who first squinted   to connect   the starry dots,
        glimpse like palimpsest   ghost images
                of scorpion   archer   fish   bear
                    chase   each   other   across   the sky?

What Was Lost

I. The Tail of the Fish Points the Way

Feng Shui practitioners used the compass as a divining tool.

Stars, compass, *shih*, divining board, small flick,
look, the tail of the fish points the way, see,
what's favorable, a sign from the gods.
Watch the turtle's head bob until it steadies,
a sign, watch the bear's tail tick through
the choices. Then point to one you will
follow, one you think you can believe in.

II. Three Days to Burn Shih's Library

*In the early seventeenth century, the Jesuits ordered
all the books on Feng Shui be burned.*

Li-Ying Shih watched as pages
of black letters marched like ants, fell
out of file, curled into smoke, drifted
into a blank sky, rained down as ash,
trash, those words that promised
to show the way, fish tail, turtle,
the twenty-four directions. Last,

carved wood plates were heaped
upon the hungry tongues

of righteousness so that
these books would never
again be printed. Never again
would the people look to the animals,
trust them to find their way.

Wind Rose

For the monks, a form of meditation, drawing a wind rose on a chart,
exacting four directions, tidy right angles, ninety degrees apart.

Lines splay a star, four winds ride the cardinal points—
N, S, E, W—each with its puffed cheeks, pursed lips, wild locks.

No compass—no skittery sliver of lodestone—sailing only by wind.
Keep the wind at your back, sailor, but when the wind dies, what then?

Carefully they draw, reach at last the far corners of the chart,
fine rays radiate from stillness at the heart, compass rose blooms,

alive in their brown cloaks billowing, their journeying out.

This World More Properly Resembles a Heart

Johann Werner's Cordiform Projection, 1514

The Earth's   not flat.
As seen from a great   height this world
more properly resembles a   heart. Parallels arc
around the central meridian—the only straight line —
all the others form a gentle curve.   If the equator's a circle,
then surely this earth must be round, and if the crust were sliced
through, a cross section—like bread—he drew what might be found.
This, the only projection drawn then, letting on the Earth is
a globe, the shape of this world—telltale heart—
might yet be cracked, every dark secret
revealed to the spinning sphere,
broken apart,
released.

Mercator Writes His Epitaph

You ask who I was? With heaven as auspice,
I espied the earth, reconciling things below with those above.

—Gerard Mercator, 1593

Cobbler's son from the lowlands, mathematician
by training, mapmaker by calling, he never went to sea.

Twenty years he dreamed how sailors and
mapmakers might chart the same flat world.

What's vexing is this: sailors sail a globe, but charts
sketched flat, how might a ship's bearing be tracked

when meridians run parallel but converge at the poles?
From magnetic north, ship's compass seeks a steady angle,

so a constant bearing scribes a gentle curve. His desire:
to spread flat the surface of the sphere. His gift

a mathematical fix: three dimensions flattened to two.
Parallels, meridians, rhumbs straightened into rectilinear trinity.

Not just through the eye of God he'd so long sought,
in reconciling the heavens above with earth below,

all of us at last could see the round world whole.

Painting of John Harrison

The Old Royal Observatory, 1766

The race is on to fix the heavens,
order the wild whirling of the stars

into seconds, minutes, hours
ticked by gears and sprockets.

Ah, the temperance of metal,
viscosity not constant but

temperamental, time ticks in fits
as honeyed oil thickens, stalls,

chill of air kisses metal parts.
Earth crosshatched in parallels,

easy to chart, world flattened
into sections, like an orange.

Sailing north and south by stars
position easily fixed, but sailing west

distance measured only in time.
The problem this: a fix will only work

if longitude is known.
Now, thanks to Harrison,

sweep of second hand marks
minutes, never mind tide set,

waves beneath the keel.
Look again. His chronometer,

too late to win, painted in
later, pocket watch fob,

its ornate scrolls, Roman
numerals, true compass rose.

His work done at last. Time
to the second, longitude found,

Earth parsed neatly into lines
running north-south, time

trapped in fishnet space,
heavens pinned down,

fixed, at last.

The Forestaff 1587

*Before the Back-Quadrants were Invented, when the Forestaff was most
in use, there was not one Old Master of a Ship amongst Twenty, but went
Blind in one Eye by daily staring in the Sun to find his Way.*

—quoted in Dava Sobel, *Longitude*

Each Noon we steady the Forestaff, squint into scratched Glass,
count how many fingers Sun has climbed Horizon's Ladder.

Isinglass darkened, but not enough to shield our Eyes,
rays of Sun fractal, spatterpaint retinas, Shutter stutters.

Light too long to emerge from dark emulsion
carries the Suns of many Noons, echoes and loops

down an endless Tunnel until Sight turns inward,
ghosting Image. *Look again,* we see Trees marching,

Grasses flowing like Waves, a Prairie opening to Stars.
Roar of the Sea before us now, we turn our eyes to the Horizon,

to History, an empty Tunnel that won't return our Stare.

The Wounded Dog Theory:
My Dog Responds

The grid's one thing, but really, the wacky ways we've made our
way.
History's stacked with stories but consider what's left out.

Those wounded dogs, for instance. Did they come with wounds
or were they wounded? Did dogs apply for this position?

Imagine the job description. *Wanted: dogs that bark only when in
pain.*
What about dogs that bark at tax collectors, bright arc of ball?

Was punishment meted if a stray let slip a yelp?
Did the ship sail in circles until the dog next cried out?

I imagine ships sailing, captains hanging on every bark:
Noon in London? Time for a walk? He must consult the chart.

I turn to my dog, read this account.
He whines in sympathy, clearly wants out.

The Statue of Flavio Gioia

Amalfi, Italy

For eight centuries, he's stood in the town square
holding in bronze hands the *bussola*

with its mysterious compass, iron magnet,
wind rose, its 360 etched degrees.

Did he invent it or just report it?
What about that comma gone missing,

the comma that would have made clear his role?
Did the townspeople care that no one knows?

Or did they just want a man from their town—
sacked by Pisa, destroyed by earthquake

and storm, then the Black Death—to claim
the glory, hold the magic box?

No matter his name, they tried them all:
Giovanni, Goia, Gisi, Ioha before choosing

Gioia, which means "joy" and who stands
forever complicit in history's backward

glance, *bussola* heavy in his hands.

Bravo Ocean

Fessenden's Radio Lab, Brant Rock, Massachusetts
December 24, 1906

Evidence just in: words can traverse
thin cable under sea. How else
to explain the odd bit of conversation
the Scots overheard? But music? Will it carry?

Fessenden raises the heavy arm
of the Edison phonogram, sets down
the thin needle, and the first notes make
their way down the coast, beneath the sea.

Who heard the opening notes of the "Largo"
from Handel's *Xerxes*, the quartermaster?
Did he call all to the bridge, turn up the transmitter
for the deckhands, the wipers, the galley crew?

Somewhere in the Atlantic, the United Fruit ships waited.
Earlier that day, the captain ordered *drop anchor*
and other ships followed, each anchor chain
clattering in its steep descent, sound carrying
hull to hull like Morse code, Marconi's stutter,

only language then spoken ship to ship.
Did Handel's notes become more resonant
traveling down the continent that dark

night? Or were they gilded by the sheen
of history, the way meaning shows up
a decade later, never while we're in it.
Call me naïve, but I want to believe

those sailors knew right then, like the soldiers
who heard the notes of "Silent Night" echo
through the still air from the German village
and joined them, the enemy, in song.

Brant Rock
December 24, 2006

Here, the rusted copper wire that grounded
Fessenden's transmitter still spreads like roots
beneath the earth. A ten-foot copper rod juts
into the sky, broadcasts the same signal

Fessenden tapped out just before he sent
those glittering notes down the coast,
through the century: Bravo Ocean —

‾... .‾. .‾ ...‾ ‾‾‾ ‾‾‾ ‾.‾. . . ‾ ‾.

34

Cow Falling, Again

after Fleda Brown

What did those fishermen think watching that cow drop
from the clear sky? And the cow: did she try to run,

spindly legs treading air, or did she let her thick body go
slack, nostrils flaring, ears pinned back?

Who was more surprised: the cow by this plummet
into a vast green pasture, or the fishermen

by a cow falling from the sky? Of course,
the old nursery rhyme comes to mind.

Did the fishermen recite it in that split
second before she splintered the deck,

uncertain sea poured in? Or did they just do
what any of us might do? Run for cover,

bow their heads, pray for an ending
they could tell at the bar, a story

even they could believe, *honest.*

Leap

This year, the custodians of time will ring in the New Year by tacking a "leap second" onto the clock to account for the slowing of the Earth's rotation.

—The Seattle Post-Intelligencer, Wednesday, December 31, 2008

Just a second. Just a
second to catch up
with Time that keeps
leaping ahead of
a lagging Earth—
and so the astronomers
admit the spinning
of this wobbly orb
is not as fast, not
so precise as
we once were
taught.

South

A body is a map, a record of long journeying and discovery, an accumulation of coordinates. . . . But no map can give us an accurate reading, and no means of navigation can assure us of where we are.

—Sheila Nickerson, *Disappearances: A Map*

Here Be Dragons

What could the maps promise with their lines
set down against a restless sea? No guarantees
of correspondence between stories smuggled home
by innocent children, given to the monks to draw.

With certainty their bold lines declared
the unknown known and where it wasn't,
Here be dragons, they wrote, choosing
to name what can't be known

so what blooms beneath the rose
becomes one more out-of-reach peach,
one more mirage on a vanishing horizon,
and what's charted another koan:

what's unknown will never be known;
in making it known, it becomes unknown.

Navigating the Body

No land in human topography is less explored than love.

—José Ortega y Gasset

Our bodies an accumulation of coordinates, paths not taken, streets pulled up short, lonely alleys, dead ends. In the dark I reach out, find crows' crooked feet, scrim of scars—*proud flesh*—read each scar, remember its time and place, its bright spurt of blood. These are the landscapes we think we know. These are the landscapes we'll never know. In the dark, we make our way, mapping and remapping the continents each night. Like Scheherazade we keep doing this; like Scheherazade, this is how we stay alive.

Terra Incognita

Beyond the horizon I dreamed I'd find what I didn't know.

How many times did I pull down the chart, unroll it, find

it blank? How to make my way back across that frozen sea,

bread crumbs swept clean by wind, cairns buried under

snow, stones carried off by ravens. No one knew what to tell

us. No one said, *Listen, you can ride out this gale.* We were

children, really. We didn't know what else to do. *I don't*

want to leave, I said, *a matter of survival.* Already our lives

were unbraiding; already you'd struck out for that far shore.

Triangulate

Take your bearing off the lighthouse
its intermittent gaze, see how its bright
hand sweeps across the sullen sea.

We triangulate to advance our course,
a third point of reference, imagine
a second light might illumine

a stalled-out heart. Rule of Threes:
the third leg steadies the stool,
third note blends the chord.

Go ahead, you think,
follow desire's seductive wink,
what can it hurt?

Then watch, one more time,
see how the blinding sweep
erases all that came before.

Deep Space

...and desire, because desire is full of endless distances

—Robert Hass, *Praise*

Your head thrown back, the night a magician's cape strewn with stars. We stand knee-deep in space, light streaming 2.3 million light years from *Aldebaron, Rigel, Vega* to find us here, to reach your jaw, clenched and working, to glisten my wet cheeks. How it finds its way through the universe, knows where to bend left, curve right, determines particle or wave. How this light arrives to find us hijacked by desire, reckoning the distance between words, deep space of silence.

Catenary

As in the line that runs between a tug and its tow, its thrumming pull. The lines of the schooner that made you swoon. Spiderweb, its taut, rain-beaded strands. Empty hammock, nail paring, cantaloupe rind. As in narrative arc. I want to be flexible, at least in theory. You never imagined yourself a rigid person. As in spiderweb, unstringing. As in bright arc of rind as it sails out the galley window. As in wake made by the schooner, leaving.

Tied, Untied

I. Square Knot

First knot learned: Not
a granny, its awkward squat,

one line up from under,
other clearly not.

The best way to join two lines,
says *Ashley's Book of Knots*

when the lines are pulled
each loop resists the other

with equal force:
a standoff.

II. Bowline

The knot learned so young:
rabbit or frog, tree or pond.
Story's the same: one line
threads out the circle,
around the tree, back down
into the loop. Pull lines tight,

bight's intact, knot holds,
won't seize no matter the load.

The only knot we can still untie.

III. Clove Hitch

def.: cloven = split, partly divided

A paradox of a knot, wrap the rail in an *X*,
around again, standing end tucks under,
pulls tight, off-kilter parallelogram.
Then I learn to throw two loops,
stack the empty circles with a twist,
slip down the post, *voila!* An *X*.
All these knots circling certainty:
this boat won't drift, this line will hold;
who'd guess it's me who's split.

IV. Ravel

def.: ravel: to confuse or complicate, become entangled

i.

If raveling is *to complicate*,
how do we un-ravel this mess we're in?
Is raveling the same as un?
Can we ravel what we've done?

ii.

If we're unraveling, were we raveled once?

If we were raveled, can we re-unravel, be re-spun?

iii.

rug slips. glass tilts. milk spilt.

iv.

Look: if *what's done is done,*

then, my love,

we're now un-

done.

V. Bitter End

Standing line,

not running.

A line not cleated,

not coiled, not flaked,

not faked, no knot.

Just end of the rope, end

of the line.

Flotsam

Did she cast him out or did he cast her? Does it matter?
Only that they both were exiled from what was never

(admit it!) a garden, and for years she bobs in the waves,
a glass ball, hollow, contained. She floats beneath

granite cliffs too steep to climb; swept out
to sea, is carried in the suck and restlessness of tides,

drifts past old landmarks, sees friends wave
from shore, their arms *X*'s against a blank sky.

She jostles the tattered coastline until she shimmers,
a genie's empty lamp, wishes spent.

He fetches up on another shore, hauls himself
out, naked. He does not look back. She thinks

how Lot's wife, fleeing, ignores God's advice.
She looks back, chooses salt, its rough lick,

its familiar crown, its endless burning blue.

Jetsam

First to go: Orange wristers, sagging at the cuffs. Leaky hip boots. Woolrich wool jacket, elbows frayed. Helly Hansen bibs, streaked with salmon blood no matter how hard I scrub. *Easy to throw.* Red hooded sweatshirt still reeks of fish, XtraTufs cut off for loafers, wool watch cap for night drifts. *Let them go.* What's harder: full volume of Conrad, silver spoon with an anchor, the deer you'd carved as a gift, its legs too thin to stand. *Stow the ring, sign the papers.* Last of all: the words I wish you'd said, the words you did.

Horse Latitudes

Becalmed in the sheets, his scent lingers,
no matter the washings. Here, no horse

to shove overboard; whistling won't
summon a shiver of wind. You watch,

think *someone else's life*, not your own. See
your wood rocking chair from Goodwill tip

off, flimsy bookshelves drift away, concrete blocks
sink. True, your life together cobbled from

what was cheap, what fit in the truck, but still
it was your life—first time you wore the lace

dress, gold ring the ticket to be, at last,
a grown-up. Look around: what else to toss?

You remember man overboard drills from summer camp:
throw what's at hand—life ring, hat —whatever floats

to mark the bobbing head last seen
before the sea snaps her green purse shut.

Remember when the ship goes down,
rescuers fix her position by the trail

of debris tracing her final, futile drift.

Equilibrate

In a breath, it happens: sea outside
becomes sea within, seawater mixing
it up in salt-soaked veins.

Cell membranes let liquids slide
until they're equal, either side.
Who knows why or when?

They say drowning is the way
to go, life slurring like a dream
from which you don't wake up.

Like that, life turns on her keel,
veers off; sea pulls up her blue sheet,
leaving the rest behind to puzzle it out:

that hasty retreat,
and what to make
of whatever remains.

Adrift

What to make, then, of all those ships found drifting, crew

gone: the *Marie Celeste* off Gibraltar, child's dress still

in the sewing machine; that schooner from Cadiz,

fire still lit in the galley stove, pot of soup over-

turned; the Norwegian sealer *Isstjernen* drifting

off Newfoundland, table set, round

globe of lamps still aglow,

guttering, life

not yet

spent.

Existence Doubtful

Most [maps] were commissioned by wealthy lords,
the study of maps being often prescribed
as a palliative for melancholy.

—Lucia Perillo,
The Oldest Map with the Name America

An easy out for mapmakers who labeled an island
E.D., existence doubtful, when they weren't sure

a landmass broke from the sea, depending
on accounts carried home by sailors,

elevations sketched on sheepskin, creased
and folded, spangled with salt and rum.

I run my fingers over the chart, want to feel
uneven contours along the coastline—

tactile as the vanishing sail of your back—note
headlands signaling landfall, not a receding wake.

Existence doubtful. How many days at sea
before I'll touch flesh, trust again

what I find? In the meantime, spirit slips
its tether, sees only empty seas ahead,

hovers over every blank space on the map.

Melancholia: *Rima Dissolutas*

How we lose the world:
colors sluiced from the day,
pinned and dripping on the line,
words porridge on the tongue,
brain in its hamster looping.

Mobius strip unfurled,
blinds pulled, path twists, way
tangled, brambles twined, no sign
marks the fork, each second hardly won.
A field mouse trapped, trembling.

Loose its talon-grip—hawk unswirled!
But hooded words won't stay,
voices remote, untwisting time.
Outside, grass blades swollen with sun
distant but real as this slow disassembling.

She Speaks in Tongues

Walk beside the ocean, *listen,* she speaks in tongues,
a strange language, sentences assembling, disassembling as each wave breaks, shattering

white syllables on an empty beach,
then the long pull as it retreats, re-
assembles consonants and vowels,

returns, whipping letters into foam
sandpipers chase at surf's lip. All day,
all night she mutters her litany of loss:

lulling lullaby of L
empty hole of O
sad susurrus of S.

All day, all night she whispers,
listen, you are here in this fleeting world
and you are alone, alone, alone.

E *ast*

When you are lost, the world becomes larger than your knowledge of it.
When you are lost, the world becomes larger.

—Rebecca Solnit, *A Field Guide to Getting Lost*

We who are blind think our horse is lost,
but all the while he is sweeping us onward like the wind.

—Rumi

Lost

That life she'd slipped on like her red sweatshirt, now she watched it shrug off, walk away. Turned her back, then, on all that blue sea, found another sea more vast. Years later, learned how painters lay down a darker color to add richness, how magenta's sheen deepens innocent green. What she couldn't see: the black dog that loped through all her days. And she, always seeking the other story, the one missing from the men's accounts. So many ways to go astray: those storm petrels that rode with them across the gulf, then flew. Were they lost, too?

Landlocked

The heart too far from water runs straight rows of corn,
    listens, all ears, for what the corn whispers,
        dreams of a clean blue horizon; forget all this green.

The heart too far from water strings dreams to the horizon,
    stomps in mud puddles, charts the ebb and flow of blood,
        flushes the toilet twice, watches the sink drain.

The heart too far from water paces snow-stopped streets,
    licks icicles, deciphers the consonants of frost,
        imagines a black river running free under ice.

The heart too far from water drifts untethered
    each night in the dark stream of dream,
        casting off again and again, never arrives.

The heart too far from water folds paper boats from poems,
    sets a candle in each, pushes them off from shore,
        beloved orphans, sets each one adrift.

Dead Reckoning

1. the determination without the aid of celestial observations of the position of a ship from the record of the courses sailed, the distance made and the known or estimated drift.
2. guesswork

What course to follow when what's reckoned

is only what can be computed, deduced,

when what counts cannot be counted,

when the questions once posed,

supposed to yield answers—presumed—

become presumptuous, when even

imagination becomes unimaginable?

When we can estimate only how far

we have drifted from that fixed star;

even the stars collide in a black abyss.

When we can no longer *bear it in mind* —

or heart—when the spinning world

becomes reduced to numbers,

not the world that once seduced.

The Coriolis Effect

A boomerang's too easy, ditto the eager dog's ball. Think osprey's slow gyre. How sand rises off the beach, cyclones in your eyes. How the earth won't stop spinning. How the osprey's wing deflects the sun. Everything swings back sooner or later. Salmon circumnavigate the sea, empty bottle rides clockwise 'round a northern ocean. Take my right arm. Who knows why left shoes land on one beach, right shoes on another? The same wind that flutters monarchs lifts each plane's wings. How we always fetch up somewhere other than we plan.

She Dreams of Great Circle Sailing

The shortest distance between two points
a line, but only if this world is flat—

as the crow flies a better measure
for where dreams venture—

soft swell of horizon, woman's breast,
lines that wander before finding home.

Not lines but curves like barrel staves
around this spinning earth follow sun's arc

across the sea. Consider star's sidereal praise,
stone's ripple, mare's tails combing empty skies.

Bend of mast, billowed sail, heart's swell,
ever out toward that curved horizon wind carries.

How will she learn to ride the swell, let the earth curve her?

Boxing the Compass

Compass of my heart,
why does your needle skitter so?
Tell me where to sail, what arc
of earth, what shore to follow.

I'd box my heart, compass my way,
steer unwavering—not let it out—
not let those Sirens hold sway
not even a dram of doubt.

Would I were sweet Penelope
patient virtue at home, not Odysseus
lashed to the mast—that's bravery?
Or better, could see clearly as Tiresias.

O heart, if you would be true
chart me a course that frees me, too.

True North

Shooting the sun at noon, sailors gain the way.
We know the sun is there, don't need sun sights.

But stars wheel 'round above, invisible by day;
by night, must be cradled in the sextant's sight.

Blue *Rigel,* steady *Vega, Aldebaran*, that red giant.
How to still their wheeling, fix them in your sights?

So what is it she wants? To orient by one star,
even in daylight? Or to keep each star in sight?

Lodestone of the heart, magnetic filings all aligned,
points true north, not swung by others' sights.

But life is short, desire long, and longing won't suffice.
Hold your course, Holly, just trust your inner sight.

Working on Deck

Coil the line down *against the sun*
   the old-timers said,
clockwise on deck,
   and ten years later
my arms still breaststroke
   the familiar movement
loop upon loop
   rolling the line a quarter turn
against kinks,
   feeling the resistance
give way in my hands,
   stiff fibers yielding:
the line knows how to lay
   if you let it.

Now all the old loops come back
   and my hands swim
down the line by heart
   and the line remembers
all its lives,
   the past firm
in its fibers,

how they intertwine
coil upon coil
circling emptiness,
all to make way for the next.

Eye Splice

Let the line untwine, split three strands,
bend back in a bight. Then, fid in hand,
pry open the braid, spring cords apart.

First strand set against the lay, next along
side, then intertwine, like my mother braiding
my hair each morning, fingers threading

by heart as I sat on the red stool, watched
cardinals arrive to feed. Let my fingers fly
until this, too, becomes habit. Let the fid

find its way into taut wound line,
as hands know the way, until lines
intertwined circle back, find they hold.

Sailing by Ravens

They have no chart, no sailing directions.
Instead three ravens to find Iceland.

—Ari Thorgilsson, *Íslendingabók*

Planks creak, sails shudder in unseen wind. At the tiller,
Floki faces astern, watches the Faroes diminish

to flat line of horizon. They ride a barrel stave of latitude,
sight each night with the *husanotra* the Guiding Star.

On the first day out of sight of the Faroes, Floki released a raven.
Lifts dark wings into an empty sky, an exclamation point,

wings off, shadows another ship's wake home.
On the second day another raven is released. Circles, a question,

lights upon the ship's mast, an answer. *On the third day,*
another raven climbed to a great height, flew off purposefully to the west.

A raven can see land ninety miles away.
Floki could see the raven to a height of 5,000 feet.

What next? Black V of wings diminishing
to a period, winging toward certainty

in bone, feather. Floki leans against the tiller,
traces faint calligraphy across the blank slate of sky.

Steering by Monarchs

She forgot the instruments and steered instead
by butterflies knowing nothing human could be that sure.

—Alison Hawthorne Deming, *The Monarchs*

Fog thick enough to lick, horizon a blanket,

pearl gleam of sun. Sure, the sea trips

the mind, conjures creatures, but what's

this dusty heartbeat of wing?

First one. Then another. And another.

How to account for this river of wings

flowing south through generations?

She watches the monarchs drift—

cloud of orange and black—

Western mind says *discount*,

but knows better than to dismiss.

She abandons the instruments,

tracks by dusty heartbeat,

joins the wavering, certain path.

Reckoning, Again

Originally, home meant the center of the world—
not in a geographical sense, but in an ontological sense.
One's home was established at the heart of the real.

—Mircea Eliade, *The Sacred and Profane*

Not where we think we'll find
it, not where we want to go. Home
to sailors an *X* on a chart,
fixes in an orange-peeled world.
Latitude and longitude render it real,
never reckoned by the heart.

Still the trembling of this heart.
Try sticks, string, cowry shells to find
our way back to where our real
life awaits, our true home
hides within this wobbling world;
don't trust slick surfaces of chart.

In fact, give up the chart.
Listen: faint *tick tick* of the heart.
Follow it, wrest the world
back; let it at last find
you, make your way home
in the soft vessel of skin. Reel

in this landscape, distant reach of real
time and place, not found on any chart.
Sing with the aborigines, who called their home
into being, chanted it out of their hearts,
strung the land with thin lines of song to find
their way, knew the intersection of this world

and the other—plumbed vertical—world
where gods passed easily, knew more real
than street grid of city map, knew all that you find
is more than you know. Even the old charts
can't navigate the wild shoals of your heart,
won't carry you across those slippery seas home

until your bones know wherever you are *is* home.
You turn at last to this, wheeling, whirled,
sailing Great Circles of the heart,
ignoring what's not real,
never glancing at the chart,
trusting wherever you find

yourself, you are real to the world.
Abandon every chart! Let the heart
wander, find her own way home.

And the Universe Curved

She looked as far as the eye can see
But the eye is a circle—poor pupil—
And the universe curved.

—Edward Hirsch,
"The Horizontal Line" from *Lay Back the Darkness*

i.

During Cook's and Bligh's time, "truth" was established when chronometers had been adjusted and all known navigational reading had been coordinated to determine position. That corrected position, at that moment, was "the truth."

ii.

The syllogism can be true but not valid.
The syllogism can be valid but not true.

iii.

During the search for the Franklin Expedition, any party finding a cairn was to dig in the ground ten feet true north to look for another passage.

iv.

The magnetic poles switch every million years.

v.

Set a camera on a tripod, point it to the heavens.
Try to fix a star.

vi.

Wave, sine, cosine. All she knows is time rolls,
tumbles at the shore.

vii.

We are sailing. We are heading for the stars.
We are always just north of where we think we are.

All the Unseen Forces

An early memory: spinning bicycle wheel, spokes *flick flick flicking* in the sun, light on liquid moving—is it water?—what beauty would become. Striped hula-hoop, wild halo of sunflower petals, steep drop of stone. When would she see it was all spinning: spinning compass, spinning globe? All the unseen forces: terns flying pole to pole, monarchs drifting down the continent, horizon folded under every wave. Lines tied and untied, knots that won't hold. A magnetic pole that shifts, true north not true at all. Only these lines to catch the world.

N *otes*

"Correcting for Variation"

Variation is the nautical term used to describe the difference in degrees between true and magnetic north. The mariner must correct for variation when setting the ship's compass course.

"Correcting for Deviation"

Deviation is the nautical term for the difference between the compass indication of a magnetic course and the actual course, usually caused by magnetic influences on the ship.

"The Compass: What Was Lost"

The information comes from Amir Aczel's book, *The Riddle of the Compass* (Harcourt, 2001). An early compass developed in China in AD 1040 was cast in iron as a fish; its head pointed south. As far as I know, there's no relation between *Shih*, the philosophy, and Li-Ying Shih, the person, though they appear together in this poem.

"Drawing the Wind Rose"

The information comes from John Goss's comprehensive book on mapmaking, *The Mapmaker's Art* (Rand McNally, 1993): "During the Renaissance … before they knew magnetic north, sailors navigated by the winds, which charts show radiating out from what came to be called the compass rose."

"The World More Properly Resembles a Heart"

Johann Werner, a German mathematician, refined a cordiform projection that was commonly used for world maps and some continental maps through the sixteenth century and into the seventeenth century. By the eighteenth century it was replaced by the Bonne projection. Johannes Stabius was the first to draw the map.

"Mercator Writes His Epitaph"

I'm indebted to Nicholas Crane's excellent biography, *Mercator: The Man Who Mapped the Planet* (Henry Holt, 2003), for the information in this poem.

"Painting of John Harrison"

John Harrison is the subject of Dava Sobel's compelling book *Longitude* (Walker, 1995), describing the race to develop an accurate chronometer that could keep time at sea, which Harrison attempted to do. This poem is based on a painting of Harrison that hangs in The Old Royal Observatory.

"The Forestaff 1587"

The epigraph comes from the rare pamphlet *Curious Enquiries* (Special Collections, Brown University Library), which was quoted in Sobel's *Longitude*.

"Wounded Dog Theory: My Dog Responds"

This theory also comes from *Longitude,* where a more detailed description can be found. Briefly, "Powder of sympathy" could heal at a distance; apply it to an article of the wounded person and it would heal the wound. But it also causes pain, so someone came up with the idea of sending a wounded dog out on the ship. On shore, the dog's owner would dip the dog's bandage in the powder precisely at noon and the dog would then yelp, letting the captain know that "the sun is upon the meridian in London."

"The Statue of Flavio Gioia"

The reference to the statue (in Amalfi, Italy) also comes from Aczel's account of the compass's development. The *Bussola* refers to the box the compass was placed in, along with the magnet and wind rose. An entire chapter in Aczel's book is devoted to the controversial role played by Flavio Gioia, and I refer readers to it for the full story on the missing comma.

"Bravo Ocean"

On December 24, 1996, the anniversary of Fessenden's transmission, National Public Radio ran a story on the first radio transmission, in which Handel's "Largo" was played. The last line is *Bravo Ocean* in Morse code.

"Cow Falling, Again"

My gratitude to Fleda Brown for her poem "Cow Falling" in her collection *Breathing In, Breathing Out* (Anhinga Press, 2002). I'd saved the same news clipping, and here she explains what happened: "There is a story of the crew of a Japanese fishing trawler picked up at sea who claimed their boat had been sunk by a cow falling out of the sky. It turns out they weren't drunk. Russian soldiers had stolen a cow out of a field and for a prank, had loaded it onto their transport plane to take back to Russia. But the terrified cow dashed madly back and forth, banging into the walls of the hold until they decided for their own safety, they had better push it out over the sea."

"Leap"

The leap second has been used sporadically at the Royal Observatory at Greenwich since 1972, an adjustment that has kept Greenwich Mean Time, the internationally agreed time, standard. Since the exact speed of the earth's rotation can't be plotted in advance, the seconds are added as needed.

"Catenary"

A catenary is the curve assumed by a line that is flexible but not stretchable and that hangs freely from two fixed points.

"Horse Latitudes"

The term originated when Spanish sailing vessels transported horses to the West Indies. Ship crews becalmed in this mid-ocean latitude would be forced to throw their horses overboard due to water shortages.

"Adrift"

The information comes from Sheila Nickerson's fascinating book, *Disappearances: A Map* (Harcourt Brace, 1997).

"The Coriolis Effect"

The effect of a force defined by Gaspard G. de Coriolis, a French civil engineer who determined that the earth's rotation deflects moving objects or air currents to the right in the northern hemisphere.

"She Dreams of Great Circle Sailing"

Due to the earth's curve, the shortest distance between two points is a curved line and must be plotted accordingly when making ocean crossings.

"Boxing the Compass"

The title comes from the traditional maritime practice of naming all thirty-two points of the compass in clockwise order, a practice that was traditionally considered part of a seaman's education.

"Eye Splice"

An eye splice forms a loop or "eye" at the end of the line. The tool used to split open the strands of the rope is called a fid and traditionally was made of wood with a metal point.

"Sailing by Ravens"

The italicized phrases in this poem are taken from the chapter on "Raven Floki" in Farley Mowat's *Westviking: The Ancient Norse in Greenland and North America* (Little, Brown, 1965). Thanks to Barbara Sjoholm for lending me her copy.

"Steering by Monarchs"

I'm grateful to Alison Hawthorne Deming for these lines, apparently based on a true story, which appeared in a poem in her collection *The Monarchs* (Louisiana State University Press, 1997).

"And the Universe Curved"

The title is taken from a line in the poem "The Horizontal Line" by Edward Hirsch in his collection *Lay Back the Darkness* (Knopf, 2003). The reference to the cairns comes from *Maps & Dreams*, an account of early polar expeditions by Hugh Brody (Pantheon, 1983). Because both parties were in a race to find the North Pole, the cairns were deliberately placed to confuse the competition.

Acknowledgments

My thanks to Floating Bridge Press, where many of these poems originally appeared in the chapbook *Boxing the Compass*, published in 2007.

"Because the Sea Never Forgets" was reproduced as a broadside as part of the 2010 Port Townsend Arts Council exhibit, *On Water*.

"Steering by Monarchs" was featured on *VerseDaily* and was reproduced as a broadside designed and illustrated by Suzanne Moore.

"Painting of John Harrison" appeared in *The Bellingham Review* (Spring/Fall 2007).

"What the Sea Takes" appeared in *Alive at the Center: Seattle*, Pacific Poetry Project from Ooligan Press (Portland State University, 2012).

"Wind Rose" was reproduced as a broadside designed and illustrated by Joe and Marquita Green and printed by The Peasandcues Press, 2008.

"The Wounded Dog Theory: My Dog Responds" appeared in *Dogs Singing: A Tribute Anthology* (Salmon Poetry, 2010).

"Working on Deck" appeared in *Pontoon 6* and *The Hedgebrook Journal 2000*.

This collection was written over many years and with the support of many; I am grateful to the following:

Deep gratitude to the University of Alaska Press for choosing this manuscript and for producing beautiful books. In particular, my thanks to series editor Peggy Shumaker and to acqusitions editor James Engelhardt for his helpful feedback and patience with my many questions. Gratitude, too, to Joeth Zucco for careful copyediting, production editor Sue Mitchell for deftly keeping the book on schedule, and Evon Zerbetz for the use of her raven image on the cover.

My gratitude for residencies at Hedgebrook, Centrum, Vermont Studio Center, and the Helen Riaboff Whiteley Center in Friday Harbor, all of which provided invaluable solitude, without which the collection would not exist. I'm also grateful for a fellowship from the Washington State Artists Trust in 2012 that allowed me to complete the manuscript.

This collection grew out of my MFA thesis at the Rainier Writing Workshop MFA program at Pacific Lutheran University, so my thanks—always—to Stan Rubin and Judith Kitchen. Deep gratitude to Peggy Shumaker, who has supported and nurtured this project for many years. Gratitude, too, to Fleda Brown, for sharing her knot poems, and to my fellow students in the first graduating class, for their camaraderie and inspiration. In particular, I want to thank Kathleen Flenniken for her careful reading, helpful comments, and for her steadfast belief in this manuscript.

Because this project spanned many years, it involved several writing groups. My gratitude to the members of the Village Idioms who responded to early drafts of these poems with their usual good humor, and to the amazing women poets on the Kitsap Peninsula who helped polish later drafts and for being willing to workshop "yet another navigation poem." I'm grateful to be part of a lively writing community, with many other friends and colleagues providing inspiration and encouragement along the way, too many to name, but I hope you know who you are; my deepest gratitude to all of you.

As always, profound gratitude to Tess Gallagher for setting me on the poetry path and steadily encouraging me along it, and for the inspiration of her work and life.

Last, my heartfelt gratitude for my husband, John, for his sharp editorial eye, steadfast patience, and steady course, and to our beloved Fox, whose unflagging spirit inspires me daily.